TALKABOUT Soil

TALKABOUT Soil

Text: Angela Webb
Photography: Chris Fairclough

Franklin Watts
London/New York/Sydney/Toronto

©1986 Franklin Watts

First published in Great Britain by

Franklin Watts
12a Golden Square
London W1

First published in the USA by

Franklin Watts Inc
387 Park Avenue South
New York 10016

ISBN: UK edition 0 86313 477 7

ISBN: US edition 0–531–10371–4
Library of Congress
Catalog Card No: 87–50232

Editor: Ruth Thomson
Design: Edward Kinsey
Additional Photographs: Zefa

Typesetting: Keyspools Ltd
Printed in Italy

About this book

This book has been written for young children – in the playgroup, school and at home.

Its aim is to increase children's awareness of the world around them and to promote thought and discussion about topics of scientific interest.

The book draws on examples from a child's own environment. The activities and experiments suggested are simple enough for children to conduct themselves, with only a little help from an adult, using objects and materials which will be familiar to them.

Children will gain most from the book if the book is used together with practical activities. Such experiences will help to consolidate knowledge and also suggest new ideas for further exploration and experimentation.

The themes explored in this book include:

Soil is made from rocks.
Soil contains water and air.
Soil contains organic material.
Soil helps plants to grow.
Soil supports life.

Have you ever done any digging?
Was the soil light and easy to dig?

Was it hard, dry and crumbly?

Or was it soft, squelchy mud?

What is soil?

Spread some soil out on paper.
What can you see?

Roots? Dead leaves? Rock?

Soil is made of tiny pieces of many things.

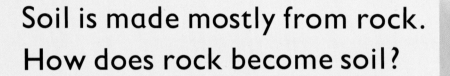

Soil is made mostly from rock.
How does rock become soil?

Take some hard clay
and rub the lumps together.
What happens?

It crumbles into tiny pieces.
Rock is broken into pieces
by rain, wind, frost …

and by rivers and streams.

Soil is not only pieces of rock. Dead plants and animals rot, and become part of the soil.

The remains of plants and creatures
add goodness to the soil.
This goodness is called humus.

Soil also has air in it.

Fill a bowl with pebbles.
Can you see the spaces between them?
Soil has air spaces in it too.

Pour water over the pebbles.

The water fills all the spaces.
Water soaks into soil in this way.

Look at these three kinds of soil.

What differences can you see?

clay soil

sandy soil

loam

Feel the difference between types of soil.

Make a ball of clay and another of sandy soil.
Poke holes in them with your fingers.
Fill the holes with water.
Which ball of soil holds water longer?

Clay soil holds water.
Fields of clay soil can easily become flooded.

Water runs quickly through sandy soil. Plants in sandy soil may not have enough water to grow well.

Plants grow well in loam.
It has the right mixture
of clay, sand and humus.

Try this experiment.

Fill three plant pots with different soils.
Plant seeds in each and water them.

Leave the pots in a light, warm place,
for about two weeks.
Water them every day.

Watch how well the seeds grow
in each kind of soil.

Farmers turn the soil over
before they sow their crops.
They turn it over to break up the lumps.
What do you think the birds are looking for?

Soil is a home for worms, wood lice
and many other creatures.
They burrow into the soil
and make spaces for air and water.

See how worms tunnel through soil.

Put layers of different soils
in a glass tank or jar.
Put in some worms and cover
with black paper.

After a few days, take off the paper.
What changes have the worms
made to the soil?

Plants which people and animals eat need soil to grow in.

We cannot live without soil.